Brat Packs

Cool Jewellery

Written by
Deri Robins

Hippo

Scholastic Children's Books,
Commonwealth House, 1-19 New Oxford Street,
London WC1A 1NU
a division of Scholastic Ltd
London ~ New York ~ Toronto ~ Sydney ~ Auckland

Published by Scholastic Ltd
Text copyright © Deri Robins 1997
Illustrations copyright © Martin Chatterton 1997

ISBN 0 590 19502 6

Printed and bound in China

10 9 8 7 6 5 4 3 2 1

The right of Deri Robins and Martin Chatterton to be identified as the
author and illustrator of this work respectively has been asserted by
them in accordance with the Copyright, Designs and Patents Act, 1988.

 When you see this sign next to an activity,
make sure you've got an adult nearby –
they do come in useful sometimes!

Contents:

In case you're sitting there wondering, here are five very good reasons why jewellery's cool, and why making your own's even better:

1. Making jewellery's fun. Loads of fun, in fact.

2. It's dead easy. You may not be able to draw a straight line, but any fool can thread a bead onto a piece of string.

3. It's cheap. Most of the things you need can be found around the home or in this pack.

4. Once you've mastered a few basic skills, you'll be able to make pressies for birthdays and Christmas for the rest of your life. It'll save you lots and lots of lovely money.

5. It'll get you noticed. Friends, family and the guy you've fancied since you were six will all be incredibly impressed with your style and originality.

Over the next few pages, you'll find out what things you need to get started, and how to use them.

Bits and Pieces

Most of the stuff you're going to need can be found around the house or in the pack supplied with this book.

You're also going to need

- a work surface – a table in your room is ideal. Sweep all the junk into a carrier bag, put it in the back of the cupboard, and protect the surface of the table with several sheets of newspaper.

- a pair of scissors

- a craft knife – you may have used one of these at school. They are very sharp, so never ever use one without a grown-up's help.

- glue – a glue stick is good for small bits of card and paper, but PVA's even better. This is astoundingly useful stuff, since it can be used for sticking, varnishing, papier mâché and even making fake stained glass (more about that later on). For fixing jewellery to findings (the metal attachments in the pack), you can use epoxy glue, which comes in a tube.

- modelling clay – you don't have to buy this, but it's useful for making home-made beads.

- flour and water – for making salt-dough (a cheap alternative to modelling clay).

- old newspapers – for covering your work surface, and making papier mâché.

- a needle and strong thread – for making necklaces.

7

- paints – thick poster paint or acrylic paint are great. Ordinary white emulsion paint makes a good undercoat (see page 11).

- thin wire – your parents may already have some in the tool cupboard. Or you might be able to get away with using paper clips instead. Otherwise, you can buy silver or copper wire from your local craft shop – you'll need 0.6mm thickness.

- junk – after reading this book, you'll realize that jewellery can be made out of almost anything. Keep a collection of cardboard, scrap paper, old sweet wrappers, bits of coloured thread, ribbon, leather thongs, elastic, shells, leaves, metal junk like washers and screws, empty cardboard rolls, kitchen foil and anything glittery or sparkly.

  Before you start an activity, read through the list of materials, and check you have everything you need.

- last but not least – a grown-up assistant. Because a trip to Casualty can seriously ruin your day, you should always have one of these to hand when you're making your jewellery – especially if you're cutting or baking.

**Here are some important things you need to
know before you go any further:**

Craft knives...

are sharp, but needn't be dangerous. Use a ruler to help you cut in a straight line, and don't press too hard – use several light strokes instead.

Papier mâché

One great way to make jewellery is to cover card shapes with papier mâché.

PVA mixed with the same amount of water is much easier than wallpaper paste. If you do want to use wallpaper paste though, just mix together one part flour to two parts water and heat in a pan.

Tear some newspaper into small strips, and brush the PVA or paste over both sides. Cover the card shapes with the strips, building up the layers, and leave to dry.

Cool tip:
Use a different colour paper for each layer – for example, you could use a pink financial paper or a comic for one layer, and ordinary black and white newspaper for another. It makes it much easier to see what you're doing.

If you glue stuff like string, lentils or bits of card
to the papier mâché before painting it, you'll get
an interesting lumpy surface...

Painting and varnishing

You can simply slosh your poster or acrylic paints
over your home-made jewellery, but you'll get
better and brighter results if you seal it with white
emulsion paint first of all.

> **Cool tip:**
> Spattering gives an unusual finish – just dip an
> old toothbrush in some fairly thin paint, and flick
> it in the direction of your jewellery. Make sure
> that you cover everything in sight with plenty of
> newspaper or very old sheets before you try this...

To protect your jewellery, brush on a final coat of
polyurethane varnish. Rinse the brush in white
spirit afterwards. If you've used acrylic paints, you
can use PVA glue instead - it dries to a clear
shiny finish.

If someone said "bead", you'd probably picture a small, round thing with a hole in the middle.

However, beads don't have to be round, or even particularly small. As far as we're concerned, a bead is anything that stays still long enough for you to make a hole through the middle! In this book we'll show you how to make beads from shells, paper, old junk and even food! Once you accept that nearly anything can be turned into a bead, you're bound to come up with loads of brilliant ideas of your own.

Craft shops sell lots of ready-made beads – these are very attractive and useful, but cost about the same as a perfectly good necklace. If you're on a super-tight budget, you could make at least some of the beads at home – as well as saving buckets of money, it means that your jewellery will be truly original. The only limits are your own imagination...

Roll-ups

You will need

-  thin card
- scrap paper (anything from old magazines to wallpaper)
-  PVA glue
- a brush
- scissors

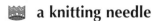

- a knitting needle

- paints and brushes

- varnish

1. Copy this triangle onto the card, and cut it out to make a template.

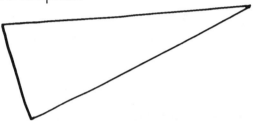

2. Trace around the template onto the paper 20 times (to make 20 beads), and cut them out.

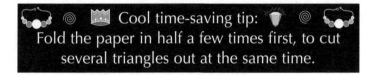

Cool time-saving tip:
Fold the paper in half a few times first, to cut several triangles out at the same time.

3. Mix some PVA with the same amount of water, and brush this mixture over both sides of a triangle. Roll it around the knitting needle to make a bead.

4. Slide the bead off the needle, and put it on a wire rack until the glue has dried.

14

5. Do the same thing with the other triangles. When they're all dry and hard, they can be painted and varnished (see page 11).

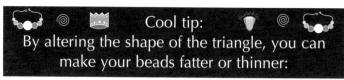
Cool tip:
By altering the shape of the triangle, you can make your beads fatter or thinner:

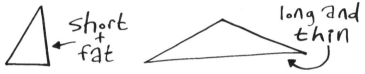
short + fat

long and thin

Beads from clay

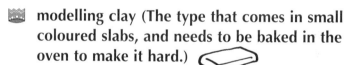

You will need

▨ **modelling clay (The type that comes in small coloured slabs, and needs to be baked in the oven to make it hard.)**

▨ **a blunt knife**

▨ **a couple of metal skewers**

1. Roll the clay into a sausage, then chop it into equal bits with the knife.

2. Roll the bits into balls, ovals or cylinders and push them onto the skewers.

15

3. Rest your clay kebabs on a baking tray, and get your grown-up helper to shove them in the oven. (Read the instructions to see how long the clay needs to be in the oven.)

4. When the beads are hard, ask your lovely assistant to take them out of the oven, and leave them to cool down.

To make square beads, just roll out the clay with a rolling pin, then chop them into cubes. These look great with letters painted on them: thread them onto a leather thong to spell out your name – or the name of someone you fancy!

Cool tip:
You can try moulding the clay into tiny birds, flowers, hearts, stars – anything else that takes your fancy!

You can also get all sorts of fab effects by mixing different colours together:

Magic marbling   ACTIVITY!

1. Roll two or three pieces of clay into super-thin

sausages, and twist them together as shown:

2. Chop into bits, and roll them into balls – the colours will blend together to make a marbly pattern.

3. Thread onto the skewer, and bake until they're hard.

Flower power

If the hippy-chick, 60s look is your thing, try this cool idea.

1. Roll out a thin sausage in one colour, then make three sausages each from two other colours.

2. Lay them together as shown.

3. Now roll out a thin piece of clay in a fourth colour, and wrap this around the others. Carefully roll this into a long rope, and cut into thin "flowers".

4. Take yet another slab of clay, and roll into balls. Press the flowers onto the surface, and roll the bead in your hand until it's smooth all over.

5. Thread onto a skewer and bake until hard.

 Cool tip:
If you made the sausages thicker, and forget about stage 4, you'll end up with a fantastic set of buttons! (More about buttons on page 44:)

Loads of dough ACTIViTY!

This bead idea really will save you loads of dough!

<u>You will need</u>

 **150 grams plain flour**

1 tablespoon salt

6 tablespoons cold water

metal skewers

paints and brushes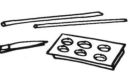

varnish

1. Stir the flour, salt and water together, then squish the mixture into a dough.

2. Knead the dough until it's smooth and stretchy. Go on, really put some effort in – you can pretend it's your little brother or sister's head!

3. Shape it into beads – as big or small as you like, as described on page 15.

4. Thread the beads onto the skewers, and bake at 170°C/Gas mark 2 for about an hour.

5. Unless you have a strange desire for grey, chalky-looking jewellery, you will want to paint your beads (see page 11). You can go for the latest wild colours – and choose something to match your favourite outfit. It's easiest to do this while they're still on the skewers – you can rest them across an open box while they're drying.

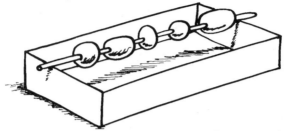

6. To make your beads shiny (and to stop the paint rubbing off on to your fave T-shirt), varnish them.

To add extra glitz and glamour, roll the beads in glitter before the varnish dries!

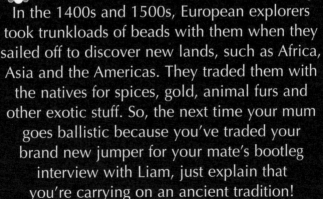

Cool fact:
In the 1400s and 1500s, European explorers took trunkloads of beads with them when they sailed off to discover new lands, such as Africa, Asia and the Americas. They traded them with the natives for spices, gold, animal furs and other exotic stuff. So, the next time your mum goes ballistic because you've traded your brand new jumper for your mate's bootleg interview with Liam, just explain that you're carrying on an ancient tradition!

Necklaces with Attitude

Fish around in the pack until you find something that looks like this:

As you've probably realized, this is a necklace clasp.

To start making a necklace, tie one end of a piece of strong thread to one side of the clasp – use a knot like the one shown below. You might be able to find thread around your house – or even in a local craft shop!

good knot for tying necklaces

Thread the other end with the needle, and push it through the beads. When the necklace is the length you want, tie the loose end firmly to the other side of the clasp. Feed both loose ends back through the beads, using the needle. Easy, huh?

Lots of identical beads threaded together look great. You could also try combining different shapes and sizes. Home-made beads can be mixed with shop-bought ones – tiny seed beads like these don't cost too much (and you'll find some smaller beads in this pack).

Lay all the beads in a line first of all, so that you can decide whether you like the finished pattern – it saves a lot of re-stringing later on.

You can easily make a double (or triple) strand, by attaching a second string of beads to the same clasp.

If you've used small beads, you could even twist or plait the strands together.

Beach baby ACTIVITY!

Why shell out your hard-earned cash when some of the best beads are for free?

Next time you're on the beach, pick out a few shell specimens (making sure they're uninhabited!) and you'll have the beginnings of some totally unique jewellery.

<u>You will need</u>

▧ **some shells**

▧ **strong thread, thin string or raffia**

▧ **a grown-up helper with a drill (using a fine bit)**

1. Persuade your grown-up helper to drill a hole through each of the shells (it helps if you wedge the shells in a piece of plasticine first).

2. Try laying out your shells in different patterns, until you stumble upon one you like.

3. Thread them together, tying a knot before and after each shell:

Or, for the ultimate beach baby look, just tie a few shells to a leather thong, and knot it around your neck, wrist or ankle. You could even make a matching set for your favourite mussel-man!

Shells look brilliant mixed with beads – try fake pearls, clear blue and green beads, or black-and-white marbled beads (see page 16).

For shell-like ears, thread some of the prettiest specimens onto earring findings – (see page 46).

If you paint the shells silver or gold, they'll look like metal.

> **Cool fact:** People have been making jewellery out of pebbles, bones and shells for a very long time. We're not talking mere hundreds of years here – necklaces like these were all the rage around 40,000 BC with the Cro-Magnons.

Dream on

If you fancy being Pocahontas for a day, sling this native North American dream catcher round your neck.

You will need

- a large ring of some kind (a thin bangle if you have one – if not, cut a ring from card)
- some raffia (from a local craft shop)
- thin string or coloured thread
- a needle
- a leather thong
- some beads, shells or feathers for decoration

1. Wind the raffia around the ring, until there are no gaps showing. Glue the ends in place.

25

2. Loop the string loosely around the ring six times, and tie the ends together. (Your loops shouldn't be quite as loose as they are here.)

3. Thread the needle, and push another length of string through one of the loops. Tie in a knot, then do the same with the other five loops.

4. Push the needle through one of the new loops, and tie a knot. Push a bead or shell onto the thread, then knot the thread onto the loop on the opposite side.

5. Do this two more times, so that each loop is linked with the one opposite. Pass the thread through the bead each time you do this.

6. Tie the thong to the ring like this:

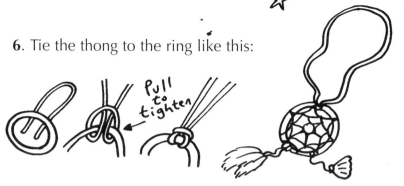

Pull to tighten

If you like, you can hang another thong from the bottom, and thread on a few beads, feathers or shells.

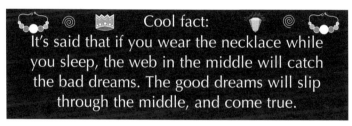
Mystic pendant

Salt-dough can look a lot like metal when it's painted so it's really good for making Celtic-style pendants.

<u>You will need</u>

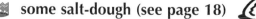
▨ **thin card**

▨ **some salt-dough** (see page 18)

▨ **a leather thong**

1. Trace the outline of this shape onto thin card, and cut it out.

2. Roll out the dough, until it's about a centimetre thick.

3. Lay the card on top of the dough, and cut out the shape with a knife. Use a knitting needle to make markings on the surface.

4. Make a hole near the top, and get your grown-up helper to bake it for you (see page 19).

5. Tie the ends of the thong together, and loop it onto the pendant:

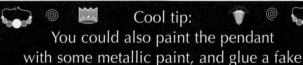

Cool tip:
You could also paint the pendant
with some metallic paint, and glue a fake
gem in the middle.

Or, if you aren't really into the Celtic look, what about one of these groovy 60s pendants?

Hippie chick daisy

Far out heart

Instead of stringing your pendants onto a thong, you could sew it to a piece of velvet ribbon to make a choker. Sew bits of Velcro to the ends to make an effective fastening.

Pasta fashion

ACTIVITY!

There's always pasta hanging around your kitchen – and it comes in all sorts of exciting shapes and sizes. So why eat the stuff when you can hang it round your neck?

You will need

- Some dried penne (or any other tube-shaped pasta)
- a couple of knitting needles or skewers
- paints and brushes

strong thread

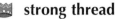

varnish

1. Thread penne on the knitting needles, and rest them on an empty cardboard box.

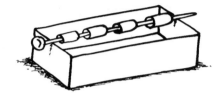

2. Paint them in jazzy colours of your choice, and varnish.

3. Thread them into a necklace – mix them with some big, round beads if you like.

Brilliant Bracelets and bangles

Bracelets are dead easy to make – just thread your beads onto thongs or elastic, and knot the ends around your wrist.

Here are a few more ideas.

Friendship bracelet

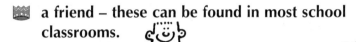
ACTIVITY!

A friendship bracelet is just a plait with attitude. There's hundreds of varieties to choose from – here's one to get you going.

<u>You will need</u>

- **a friend – these can be found in most school classrooms.**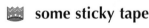

- **five thick pieces of thread – wool, thick string or embroidery thread all work well.**

- **some sticky tape**

1. Cut the threads into 40cm lengths.

2. Knot the five threads together, leaving about 10cm above the knot.

3. Tape the knotted end to your work surface.

4. Take the thread on the far right, and weave it through the others as shown. Give it a fairly firm tug.

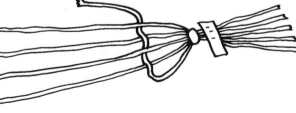

5. Now do exactly the same with the next thread on the right:

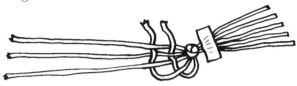

6. Keep plaiting away until you're 10cm from the end, then knot the ends together.

7. Grab a friend, and tie the bracelet around her wrist.

If you like, you could thread a couple of beads or shells onto the ends before tying.

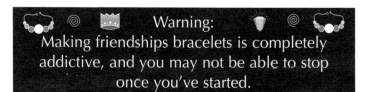

Warning:
Making friendships bracelets is completely addictive, and you may not be able to stop once you've started.

Egyptian-style bangle

If you're cross-eyed with all that plaiting, here's a snaky Egyptian bangle to make from everyone's favourite piece of junk – the empty kitchen roll.

You will need

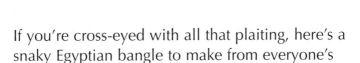

- 🟫 **the empty kitchen roll**
- 🟫 **scissors**
- 🟫 **thin card**
- 🟫 **PVA glue**
- 🟫 **gold or silver paint**
- 🟫 **a brush**

1. Cut the kitchen roll into a spiral, and cut the ends into a round shape.

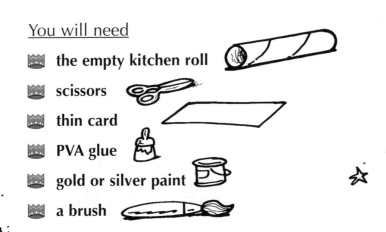

2. Cut shapes from thin card, and glue these to the bangle.

3. Paint it silver or gold.

Cool tip:
To make the bangle look like it's made of studded metal, glue on some lentils before paintings. Or, for a glitzy disco look, glue on lots and lots of shiny sequins after the paint has dried.

To make a snake bangle, cut a tail at one end, a head at the other and paint on some eyes.

Cool fact:
The queens of ancient Egypt may have worn cool jewellery, but some of their other ideas were pretty weird. Did you know, for example, that they always wore fake beards during important court functions?

RINGS 'n' THINGS

Run rings around your mates with these cool ideas. We'll guarantee you'll have the best dressed hands for miles! Rings can be as sensible or as silly as you like...

Make priceless jewels from clay or dough – roll out the shape you want, flatten the bottom slightly, and bake as usual. Stick the bead to one of the rings in your pack with epoxy glue.

Look for likely "jewels" in your local sweetie shop – liquorice allsorts and love hearts can be varnished with PVA, and glued to your ring.

When you've used up the rings in the pack, you may like to try something slightly different...

Pulp fashion

<u>You will need</u>

- **some thin card**
- **scissors**
- **masking tape**
- **newspaper**
- **PVA glue**
- **paints and brushes**
- **your finger**

1. Cut the thin card into a thin strip, and curl it around your finger.

2. Tape the ends together – make sure you can slip the ring on and off your finger.

3. Cover both sides of the ring with two layers of papier mâché.

4. To make "jewels", just scrunch up small pieces of paper. Tape them to the ring, and cover the whole thing with an extra layer of strips.

5. Leave in a warm place until the ring has dried hard, then paint and varnish.

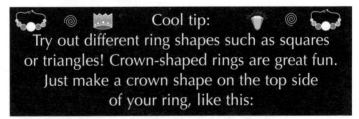

Cool tip:
Try out different ring shapes such as squares or triangles! Crown-shaped rings are great fun. Just make a crown shape on the top side of your ring, like this:

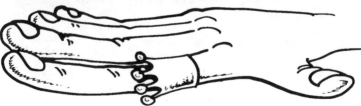

Use empty sellotape rolls in the same way, to make bodacious bangles!

Twister

You will need

- some modelling clay – metallic colours look great.
- a ring that fits your finger.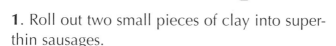

1. Roll out two small pieces of clay into super-thin sausages.

2. Twist the sausages together. Curl into a circle (using your ring as a size guide), and pinch off the loose ends. Join the ends by pressing them firmly together.

3. Disguise the join with a "jewel" made from clay. (If this falls off during baking, just glue it back on later.)

4. Bake in the oven.

Cool fact:
Which finger do you wear your ring on? It may (or may not) surprise you to learn that in 17th-century England, women wore their wedding rings on their thumbs.

Remember to check out the following badge ideas, and make smaller versions for your rings.

Badges, Brooches and Other Baubles

Badges and brooches are dead easy to make. You can simply cut a shape from thick card, paint and varnish it, and glue it to one of the badge pins in this pack.

But you can do much, much better than that...

Basic badge

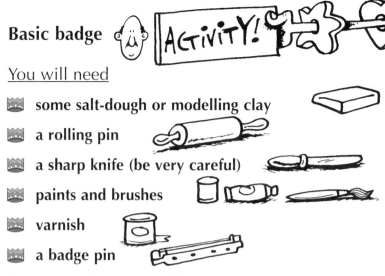

<u>You will need</u>

- **some salt-dough or modelling clay**
- **a rolling pin**
- **a sharp knife (be very careful)**
- **paints and brushes**
- **varnish**
- **a badge pin**
- **epoxy glue**

1. Roll out the clay or dough, until it's about half a centimetre thick.

2. Cut out some shapes. You could make templates from card first, and cut around them with the knife. Or use pastry cutters to stamp out hearts, stars and animal shapes.

3. Make your badge more interesting by moulding a few extra details from dough. Dab the joins with water to help the bits stick together. If they fall off during cooking, just stick them back on again before painting.

4. Bake as described on page 19.

5. When the badges have cooled down, paint both sides in your brightest, brilliantest colours.

6. Varnish the badges and stick the pin to the back with epoxy glue.

Use permanent markers or metallic felt-tips to make badges with attitude.

Cool tip:
Make flowers by overlapping petals cut from dough, and put a small blob in the middle to cover the joins.

You can use all kinds of stuff to decorate your badges. Try using metal washers, buttons, foreign coins, paper clips, interesting pasta shapes, lucky charms from a cracker, you name it – then paint the whole thing silver or gold.

Dangle small shapes from bigger ones. Make holes with a knitting needle before baking, and link the two shapes together with thin wire or thread.

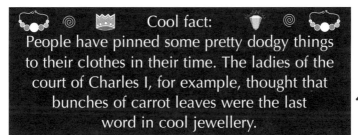

Cool fact:
People have pinned some pretty dodgy things to their clothes in their time. The ladies of the court of Charles I, for example, thought that bunches of carrot leaves were the last word in cool jewellery.

Baby, it's you!

If you want to keep your loved-one close to your heart, try this sweet idea.

You will need

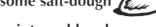

- a small photo – this could be you as a baby, your mum, or a pic of your fave megastar cut from a magazine.

- some salt-dough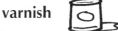

- paints and brushes

- varnish

- something over-the-top for decoration – for example, red glitter, stick-on jewels,

43

coloured foil from sweetie wrappers, fake
pearls, sequins, etc, etc.

 a badge pin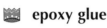

 epoxy glue

1. Roll out the dough until it's about 1cm thick,
then cut out a shape – squares, hearts and ovals
look good.

2. Lay the photo in the middle, and gently press it
into the dough. Take it out, and bake the shape as
usual.

3. Paint the badge, then glue the photo back in
place. Give the whole thing a coat of varnish.

4. Glue on all your over-the-top decorations.

5. Glue the badge finding to the back with epoxy
glue.

Button it!

Big, beautiful buttons can turn a boring old piece
of clothing into a totally amazing new outfit:

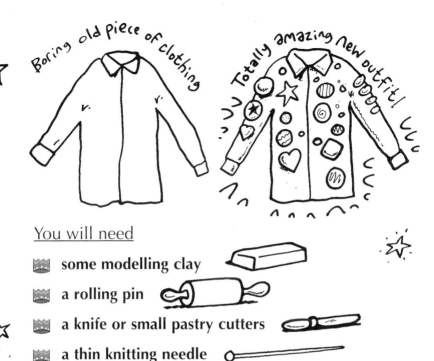

Boring old piece of clothing

Totally amazing new outfit!

You will need

- some modelling clay
- a rolling pin
- a knife or small pastry cutters
- a thin knitting needle

1. Roll out the clay until it's about half a centimetre thick.

2. Cut out some buttons, using the pastry cutters or a knife (you could make a template from card first of all).

3. Make 2, 3 or 4 holes in each button with the knitting needle.

4. Bake as shown on page 16. (Warning! These buttons may not survive a trip through the washing machine.)

Easy Earrings

This pack contains a set of clip-on earrings, as well as findings for pierced ears. Here's how you use them.

Pierced ears

Findings for pierced ears come in two bits.
There's the hook, which goes through your ear...

and the pin, which looks like this:

Thread your beads onto the pin, and use tweezers
to make a small loop at the top. Thread this loop
onto the hook, and close up the gap. If this all
sounds a bit fiddly, get your grown-up assistant to
help you.

press to close

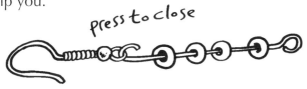

Clip-ons

To use the clip-on type, just stick them to the
back of the earrings with epoxy glue.

That's all you need to know about making
basic earrings. Simple, eh?
Or, if you've used earring pins, hook them onto
the little ring at the bottom.

Megalobes

These super-light earrings look big and dramatic, but won't drag your earlobes down to floor-level.

You will need

- **bits of card**
- **scissors**
- **old newspaper**
- **varnish**
- **paints and brushes**
- **earring findings**
- **epoxy glue (for clip-ons only)**

1. Draw one of these shapes onto the card, and cut it out. Draw around the first shape to make the second one.

2. For pierced ears only, push the straight end of a pin into each piece of card (you don't need to do this if you're using clip-ons).

48

3. Cover both sides of the card with two layers of papier mâché, and leave to dry.

4. Paint the earrings, and varnish.

5. For pierced ears, attach the pins to the hooks.

Otherwise, glue the earrings to clip-on findings.

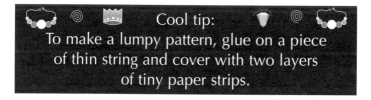

Cool tip:
To make a lumpy pattern, glue on a piece of thin string and cover with two layers of tiny paper strips.

Glue paper roses (page 56) to a pair of leaf-shaped earrings. String two or three shapes together with gold thread or thin wire.

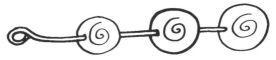

Glitz things up with squiggles made with a gold felt-tipped pen – or glue on glitter, foil sweet wrappings, fake gems, pearls or sequins...

Lucky stars  ACTIVITY!

If astronomy's your thing, try these star-studded earrings.

You will need

- salt-dough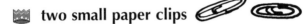
- two small paper clips
- a grown-up helper
- gold or silver paint
- a brush
- earring findings

1. Check the chart to find out which charm goes with your zodiac sign. Make the charms from salt-dough.

STAR SIGN	LUCKY CHARM
Aries	
Taurus	
Gemini	
Cancer	

Leo
Virgo
Libra
Scorpio
Sagittarius
Capricorn
Aquarius
Pisces

2. Push a paper clip into the top of each charm, then bake and paint in the usual way.

3. Hook them onto your earring findings.

4. Dangle lucky charms from ears. Make a wish – it might just come true!

Stained glass

ACTIVITY!

Follow these instructions and you could have a pair of stained-glass windows dangling from your ears!

You will need

 thin wire

■ **a grown-up helper with a set of pliers**

■ **PVA glue**

■ **a few drops of food colouring**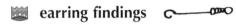

■ **earring findings** ○—◦◦○○

1. Ask your grown-up helper to cut the wire into two 6cm lengths. Twist them into two loops like these:

2. Mix a little PVA with a drop of food colouring.

3. Dip the loops into the mixture, so that the glue forms a film across the surface. Fight the temptation to blow bubbles.

4. Rest the wire rings on the side of an upturned cup, and carefully weigh down the loose end.

5. When the glue dries, it'll look like coloured glass. Make a loop at the top of the wire, and hang from your findings in the usual way.

Still stuck for presents and things to wear on special days?

Love crazy

Wear your heart on your sleeve (or dangling from your ears) this Valentine's Day.

<u>You will need</u>
- thin card
- paints and brushes
- varnish
- earring findings

1. Trace this heart onto card.

2. Now draw a chunky letter "I", about the same size as the heart.

3. In the same style, spell out the name of the person you've been lusting after for the last six months – make sure the letters all touch each other.

4. Cut out the pieces, and paint them bright pink (or red, gold, purple or whatever). Seal with a coat of varnish.

5. Make holes in the shapes as shown. Link the "I" and the heart with a small piece of wire, and hang this from one of the metal findings. Hang the other piece of card from another finding.

If you want to be his candy girl, glue a love heart sweetie to a pair of clip-on findings.

Cool for mums

Nine out of ten mums said they preferred this cool brooch to a soppy card and a bunch of daffs on Mother's Day.

<u>You will need</u>

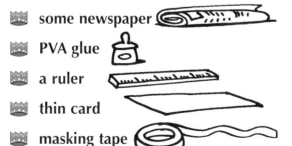

- some newspaper
- PVA glue
- a ruler
- thin card
- masking tape
- paints and brushes
- varnish

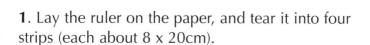

1. Lay the ruler on the paper, and tear it into four strips (each about 8 x 20cm).

2. Mix a little PVA with the same amount of water, and brush the mixture over one of the strips. Fold it in half, then brush both sides with glue.

3. Start rolling up the strip – quite tightly to begin with, then more loosely as you go along. Pinch the bottom together as you do so.

roll up loosely into rose

4. Make two more roses in the same way, and make a couple of buds by rolling smaller strips tightly.

5. Cut a square from thin card, about 8cm all round. Curl the points around, and glue the front together like this:

curl points in

Fix with tape

Hold the join together with masking tape.

6. Cover the outside of the posy with two strips of

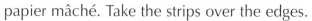

papier mâché. Take the strips over the edges.

7. Finally, brush the fourth strip of paper with glue, and fold it in half. Brush and fold again, then wrap it round the posy and tie in a knot.

Pinch bottom together

8. Leave everything to dry in a warm place – the airing cupboard's perfect.

9. Paint all the bits when they're dry. Glue the flowers into the posy, and varnish.

10. Glue a badge finding to the back.

Make dad glad

ACTIVITY!

Well, you could make him a diamond tiara, but he'd probably prefer this groovy pair of cufflinks on Father's Day:

<u>You will need</u>

- **some clay or salt-dough**
- **two split pins (paper fasteners)**
- **paints**
- **varnish**

1. Make two beads from the dough or clay (see page 18). These could be round, square or something to do with his fave hobby or interest.

Football crazy

angler

couch potato

golfer

2. Press the heads of the split pins into the base of the beads. Bake in the oven, as described on page 19.

3. Paint and varnish.

> Cool tip:
> If he's not the cufflink type, give him a keyring. Make a bead from clay or dough, and push in a paperclip before baking. Paint as usual, then slip the paperclip onto a plain keyring (you can get these from shoe repairers).

For a pretty funky bowtie, roll out some clay or dough, and cut a bow shape. Make a hole at each end before baking. After painting, cut 25 centimetres from round black elastic, thread it through the hole, and knot the ends together.

Ghoul jewellery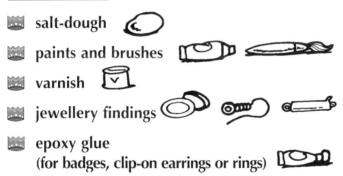

How about some wicked-looking jewellery for Hallowe'en? It'll spook your mates – but they'll also be dead envious.

<u>You will need</u>

- salt-dough
- paints and brushes
- varnish
- jewellery findings
- epoxy glue
  (for badges, clip-on earrings or rings)

1. Model the dough into the spookiest shapes you can think of.

To make the skull's eye and nose sockets, press the end of a paint brush into the dough before baking.

2. Push a paperclip in the top (for pierced ears or necklace charms).

3. Bake and paint the dough, varnish and attach to findings.

> **Cool fact:**
> 1 November is known as "The Day of the Dead" in Mexico. Skulls and skeletons are made out of all kinds of materials, including papier mâché, metal and sugar. We celebrate the evening before and see it as a scary, ghoulish celebration, but the Mexicans see it as a happy time when long dead relatives come to pay a visit!

And remember, you can make spectacular jewellery for Christmas too! But instead of skeletons, try making something a bit more friendly ... like a snowman!

Is it a card, or is it a present?

ACTIVITY!

This is a great way to give your earrings to your friends and family.

- a pair of your fabulous home-made earrings
- thin card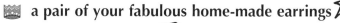
- a front-view photo of the person you've made the earrings for (or cut a pic of her fave pop star out of a magazine)
- a grown-up helper with a photocopier
- a darning needle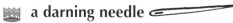
- glue

1. Ask your grown-up helper to photocopy the picture – you may need to blow it up a bit.

2. Fold the card in half, and glue the photocopy to the front. You can show the whole face, or crop in close...

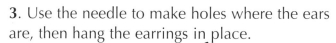

3. Use the needle to make holes where the ears are, then hang the earrings in place.

Design your own jewellery, that's what!

Grab a sketch book and pencil, and visit your local museum – or check out the library for books on ancient civilizations. The Romans, Greeks, Egyptians and Celts may have been dead for hundreds of years, but they can still teach us a thing or two about jewellery. Using the techniques in this book, you'll easily be able to fake your own copies from dough, clay and papier mâché...

Try window-shopping in trendy jewellery stores, and rip off their best ideas. Glossy fashion mags are a good source of ideas, too.

Junk shops, charity stores, jumble sales and boot sales are full of old stuff that you can recycle. Anything from a toy aeroplane to a small plastic model of the Eiffel Tower can be turned into cool jewellery – the trick is keeping an open mind!

PS. If your nearest craft shop is miles away and you need to send off for extra jewellery findings, here's a handy address. They'll send you a catalogue (which will cost you £3.50) and you can order beads and other jewellery bits. It's also much more exciting getting stuff through the post!

Write to:

Creative Beadcraft
Denmark Works
Beaumond End
Nr Amersham
Bucks, HP7 0RX